In years ahead, I hope you will share my paraphrase
of Bill Smith's Oxford poem:
Gainesville in spirit still remains;
The campus lifting from the plains
I see again in my mind's eye,
All the clearer as years go by,
And I'd have you all see it tonight,
Rain-washed in early summer light,
As limpid and as close to heaven
As each of us remembered it then.

President Robert Q. Marston, April 1984

THE
UNIVERSITY
OF
FLORIDA

Photography by Tommy Thompson

HARMONY HOUSE
Publishers Louisville

Executive Editors: William Butler and William Strode
Library of Congress Catalog Number: 90-81396
Hardcover International Standard Book Number 0-916509-69-9
Printed by D. W. Friesen, Manitoba, Canada
First Edition printed Fall, 1990 by Harmony House Publishers,
P.O. Box 90, Prospect, Kentucky 40059 (502) 228-2010 / 228-4446
Copyright © 1990 by Harmony House Publishers
Photographs copyright © 1990 by Tommy Thompson

INTRODUCTION

By Dr. Samuel Proctor
Distinguished Service Professor of History and University Historian

The date on the University's seal, 1853, marks the beginning of state support for the East Florida Seminary in Ocala, the earliest parent of the University of Florida.

The Seminary was started first as a private school to educate children from the town and nearby plantations. The local folks were happy to have the state take over financial support and transferred all the school's assets and property. These included sixteen town lots valued at $200 each, three frame buildings worth $3,800 and $1,600 in cash. Gilbert Dennis Kingsbury, founder of the school and a New England native, was appointed the first principal. The Seminary operated spasmodically during the Civil War and was moved to Gainesville in 1866. The campus site on Northeast First Street is marked by a historical plaque.

The three other parents of the University included the Florida Agricultural College, the land grant institution in Lake City, established in 1884; the South Florida Military College, a private shool that was taken over by the state in 1895in Bartow; and the St. Petersburg Normal and Industrial School which began receiving state funds in 1901.

A new era in the history of higher education in Florida began when the legislature convened in Tallahassee in April 1905. After lengthy debate, the lawmakers enacted the Buckman Act. It created the University of Florida for white male students. The Act also created a school for women, the Florida Female College. This name changed to Florida State College for Women and later to Florida State University.

The Buckman Act authorized a five-member Board of Control, appointed by the governor, to locate the new schools. Several communities in east Florida wanted the University of Florida, but the leading contenders were Lake City and Gainesville. The Tampa Tribune enthusiastically supported Gainesville, noting that the community possessed "school spirit, good water and a healthful climate." It was also "a town without a saloon or a disorderly house, and with a standard of morality that makes it an ideal college town." However, a Lake City paper described Gainesville as a "jerk-water" town whose water was not an "antidote for Gainesville fever."

To win the University, Gainesville offered for its campus a tract of 517 acres one mile west of town. It would pave Alachua Avenue (now University Avenue), the narrow rough road leading out to the University, and provide inexpensive housing until dorms were ready. Joining with the Florida Methodist Conference, the city agreed to buy the Seminary's property for $70,000. This money was used to help pay for constructing the first three buildings — Thomas, Buckman and Machinery Halls. As another lure, the city also agreed to "furnish water to the University without charge."

A wildly cheering Gainesville crowd greeted the news when it was telegraphed from Tallahassee that it would get the University. Church bells and mill whistles rang all over town. A torch light parade wove through downtown streets. According to one observer, "There was a display of fireworks, and a general love feast, and hallelujah."

Dr. Andrew Sledd was appointed president at an annual salary of $2,250. The vice president and head professor of English, Dr. James Farr, received $1,500 for his services.

Since it would take time to prepare the new campus, classes met at the Florida Agricultural College in Lake City during the academic year 1905-1906. Disappointed over losing the University, the people in Lake City were not very cooperative. They tried to stop the transfer of books, scientific equipment, and farm implements with a legal restraining order and then a civil suit, but they were not successful.

Classes started on the campus in Gainesville, September 26, 1906. There were 102 students, including thirty-eight "sub-freshmen" (students taking courses that they needed to meet admission requirements).

Dedication day, September 27, was a great time in Gainesville. The town was decorated with orange and blue banners and ribbons, the school's new colors. Nathan P. Bryan, chairman of the Board of Control and later United States Senator, delivered the main address and set forth the University's goals: to provide worthy young men with "a first class University education" and to "assist in the development of Florida's resources" so that the state might realize its great potential. A newspaper called the affair an "occasion the like of which was never before in this city."

Eighty-five years have passed since that exciting day. There have been many changes in Florida, in Gainesville, and at the University. There were fewer than 600,000 people living in Florida in 1906. That number has now increased to some 12,000,000, and Florida is counted as the nation's fourth largest state. Many new communities, a more broadly-based economy, and a more democratic political system have brought dramatic changes to the people of Florida. And the changes and growth of the University also have been phenomenal.

The student body is more than 34,000, and it is no longer only white and male. There are many Blacks, Hispanics and Asian students and faculty members. Females constitute almost one-half of the student body and in some colleges and departments they outnumber the men. In 1906, in addition to the president and vice president, the administrative staff included a librarian, physical director, auditor-bookkeeper, a stenographer and the matron, Mrs. S. J. Swanson, who was in charge of the dining room and dormitory maintenance. She and her family lived in a tiny apartment in Buckman Hall. President Sledd and his family also lived on campus. The faculty numbered fifteen. There were no deans until 1910 when the first four colleges — Arts and Sciences, Agriculture, Engineering and Law — were created.

Faculty salaries were the lowest of any state university in the South and one of the poorest in the country, and this problem persisted for many years. The professors had many responsibilities beyond their twenty to twenty-five hours weekly teaching load. They advised students, served on committees, and assisted in the library and with the athletic teams, both as coaches and players.

The changes on the campus over the years since 1906 have been dramatic as shown by the spectacular photographs in this volume. Where once there were pine forests, and later grazing pasture for cattle and farm land for the College of Agriculture, there are now scores of buildings. The trees are still there, shading walkways and roadways, playing fields, parking garages, stadiums, swimming pools, libraries, museums, gardens and lots and lots of students. Most of the structures are red brick and are in the Collegiate Gothic style as specified in the original campus plan.

The core of the campus is an open quadrangle, later named the Plaza of the Americas. Four classroom buildings — Peabody, Floyd, Flint and Anderson — were constructed at each corner. These buildings survive and are being rehabilitated for classrooms, laboratories, faculty offices and auditoriums. Two other historic buildings were demolished. Benton, the first engineering building, was replaced by Grinter, the International Studies building and Machinery Hall is now the site of Turlington Hall. The auditorium was built at the south

end of the Plaza in 1925, replacing a smaller structure now called the Women's Gym. To mark the institution's early beginnings in Ocala, the Century Tower was erected in the 1950s. It contains a forty-nine-bell carillon, specially cast in Holland, that rings on the quarter hour. The Auditorium has been used for graduations, presidential inaugurations, classes, theatrical productions, pep rallies, weddings, symphony concerts and lectures. Robert Frost was often on campus and annually read his poetry in this building.

From the beginning there was strong support for athletics at the University. It was always great to be a Gator. The Athletic Association was organized in 1904, and hired Marvin Orestes Bridges, a Cumberland University graduate, to coach football, baseball, basketball and track for an annual salary of $650, plus room and board. After only two months, Bridge's contract was cancelled when the Association found it could not "afford the heavy cost." Bridges settled for $220.75.

J. A. Forsythe, Jr., nicknamed Pee Wee, was the first coach on the Gainesville campus. The first game played in Gainesville was a victory, 6-0, over Rollins College of Winter Park. Coach Forsythe played end. Florida was not so lucky in a later match against Rollins that same season, losing 5-0. The Gator's most historic victory was over Florida Southern in 1913 with a score of 144-0. There were some bad, even calamitous, years, however. In 1916, Florida lost all five games that it played and scored only three points all season. The 1946 season was also a disaster; Florida lost nine games. When a reporter asked Coach Ray Wolf about the situation, he retorted, "It could be worse. We could have had ten games scheduled."

There were many winning years, however, with outstanding teams coached by Bob Woodruff, Ray Graves, Doug Dickey and Steve Spurrier, Florida's only Heisman Trophy winner. The great prize, the SEC Championship, continues to elude the Gators. They had a sensational season in 1984, and their 9-1-1 record awarded them the prize for which everyone had been yearning. The lament "Wait Until Next Year" was changed to a wildly enthusiastic "This is the Year of the Gator." Then came the disastrous NCAA penalties and by the spring of 1985 the decision was to deny the Gators their championship. Florida refused to return the trophy, and it is proudly exhibited on campus. Under Coach Spurrier the Gators triumphed in 1990, but additional penalties again denied Florida the coveted championship. In their hearts, though, all Gators know which is the best team.

Beginning with Andrew Sledd, the University has had a succession of presidents whose administrative skills have carried the institution through times of both trial and national and international recognition and esteem. These include Albert A. Murphree, John J. Tigert, J. Hillis Miller, J. Wayne Reitz, Stephen C. O'Connell, Robert Q. Marston, Marshall M. Criser and John V. Lombardi, who was inaugurated as the ninth president on October 12, 1990.

Two world wars, the tragic flu epidemic of 1918, the Great Depression of the 1930s and student protests that have varied from the panty raids of the 1950s to the more violent reaction to the Vietnam War in 1972, have not deterred the University's growth and development. Coeducation and racial integration changed the University in many positive ways. With its huge enrollment the University is one of the largest public universities in the country. It ranks among the top five in the number of its National Merit Scholars, and its faculty includes internationally recognized scientists and humanists. In 1985 it was invited to join the prestigious Association of American Universities and is one of only fifty-eight members in North America.

"The welfare of the state rests on the character of the people." This is the motto of the University of Florida. Providing for the well-being of Florida's and the nation's citizens has been the institution's primary objective. From its very humble beginnings 133 years ago, the University's faculty, staff, administrators and students have given of their hearts and minds to build a University that serves the state, the nation and the world.

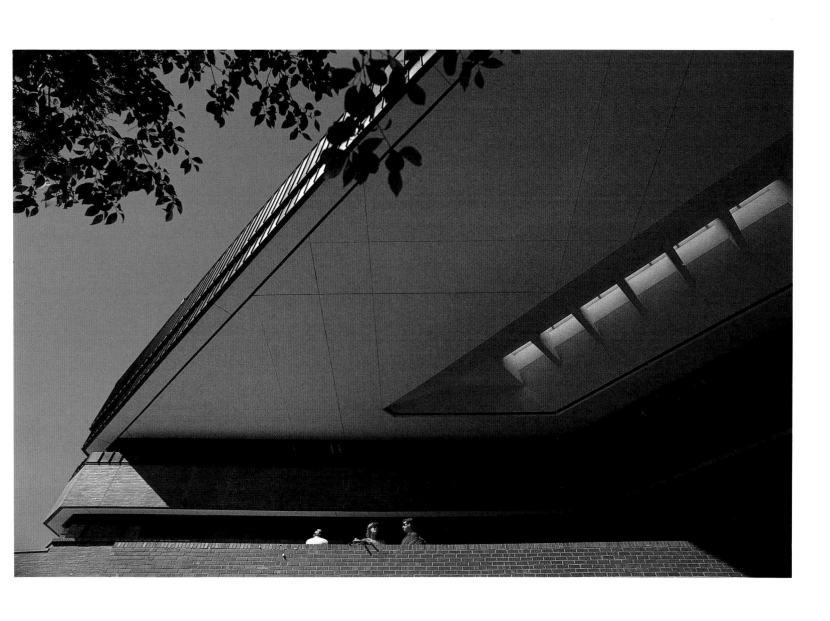

Library East

We have an opportunity to be a national top-10 public university because we come somewhat late in the game. We come after Berkeley has made mistakes, and UCLA has screwed up, and Michigan's getting tired and Hopkins is over-extended, and Columbia is running into deficit. We come at a time when we know what needs to be done in a new academic environment. The University of Florida is just starting in this game. It's the first round, and the University of Florida is doing spectacularly.

President John V. Lombardi, March, 1990

It seems to me that what you've got is a university on the move. It's an exciting place.

President John V. Lombardi, November 15, 1989

The instructor must be in touch with his students if he is to influence them and guide and incite them. But he cannot get in touch, if he has lost the capacity for enjoyment and the genuine warmth of sentiment which go with youth . . . It is the character of the instructor rather than what he teaches that affects the after-life of a student.

President Albert A. Murphree, Inaugural Address, 1909

Lake Alice

An appreciation of history involves understanding that what looks so important today . . . for instance a football or basketball game. . . might not be so important tomorrow. When you look back at this university 26 years from now, what you most likely will remember will be the lessons you learned and those who taught you . . . your professors and your classmates.

David Lawrence, Commencement, December, 1989

Gator Pond, Stadium Road

Flint Hall

Higher education must also give greater attention to the arts and to the finer expressions of the human mind and the human soul. The mind of man must be conditioned to love the finer things of life. This can come about only as our leaders, who are conditioned in our institutions, have the proper appreciation and love for the artistic and aesthetic expression of man.

President J. Hillis Miller

Preceding Page:
Law School, Commons Area

Fine Arts, Music Building

43

When the University was admitted to the Association of American Univer-
sities this spring, it marked a coming of age of higher education in Florida —
the first time any university in our state was so recognized for excellence in
its academic programs. And it was fitting that such an honor came to the
university which bears the name of our state — The University of Florida.

Chancellor Charles B. Reed, Commencement 1985

Library West, Plaza of the Americas

It is here that a dedicated and extraordinarily qualified faculty teach, conduct research, and render public service. But a great comprehensive research university is more than the sum total of its colleges. Part of that greatness is the ability to cross the boundaries of individual academic disciplines to make available the expertise in law to journalism, engineering to medicine, business to liberal arts and sciences, architecture to agriculture. The advantage of being a comprehensive university is one of our true contributions to Florida.

Inaugural Address of President Marshall M. Criser,
February 16, 1985

J. Wayne Reitz Union

Our first memories will be of fellow students, a hallowed professor or two, perhaps many more, and of a special niche or corner of this beautiful campus. That's as it should be.

President Robert Q. Marston, Commencement 1984

President's Home

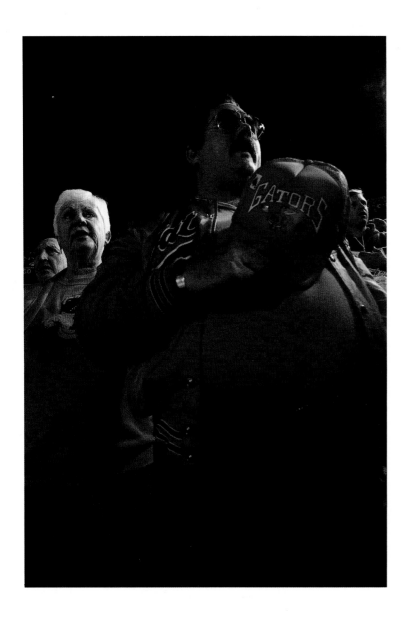
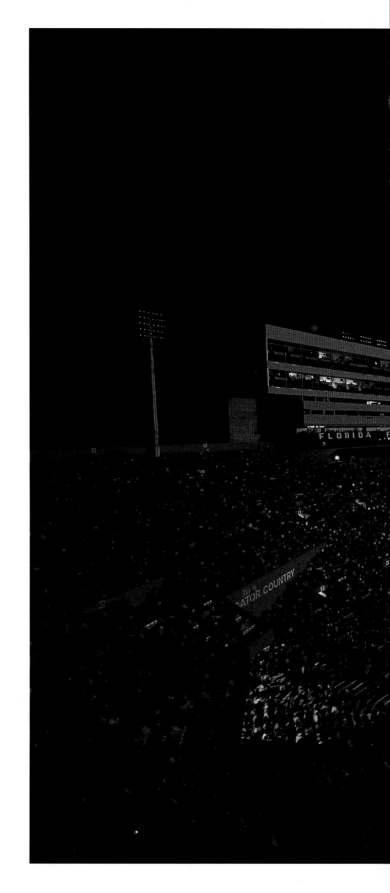

1989 Gator Growl Fireworks

Tail-Gator party after a football game

61

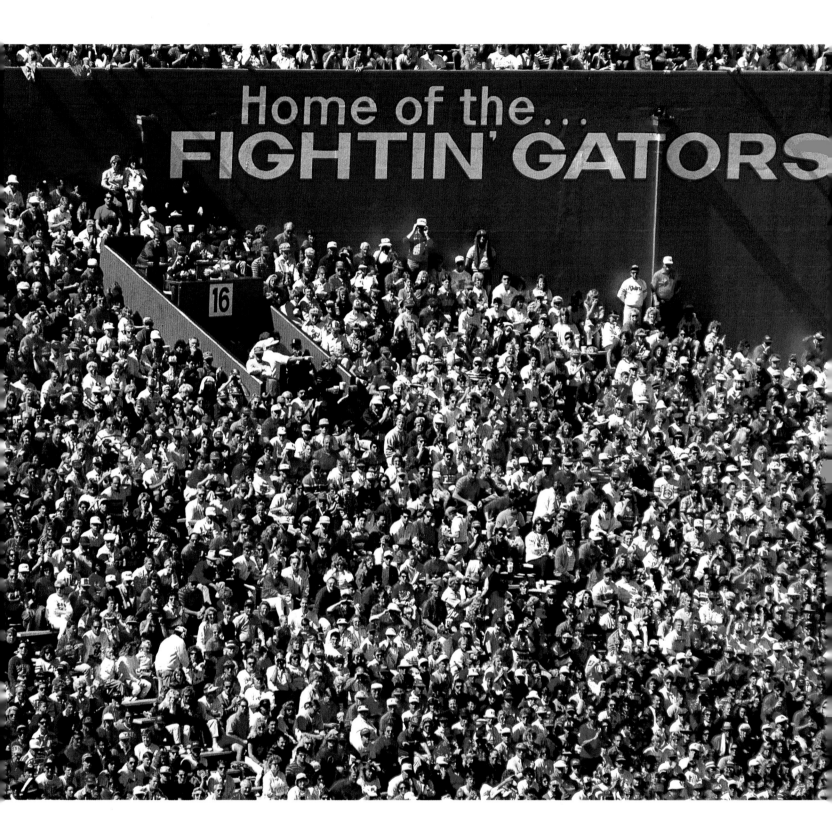

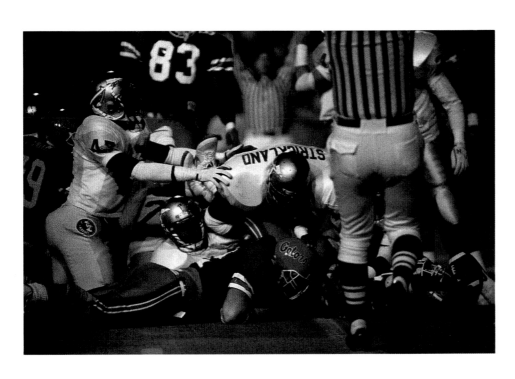

University Auditorium and Century Tower

Ben Hill Griffin, Jr. Medical Research Building

When I came here in 1948, Gainesville was a sleepy little college town of 24,000. There were even railroad tracks running up the middle of Main Street. The University had 11,000 students . . . a third of its present size. No one could have accused it of being a "research center." Research was not exactly frowned on, but it was something you did in your spare time, like chasing butterflies on Sunday afternoon.

What a change 33 years have made. Your University is now one of the nation's major research institutions.

Dr. Alex G. Smith, University of Florida Distinguished Alumni Professor, Commencement, August, 1981

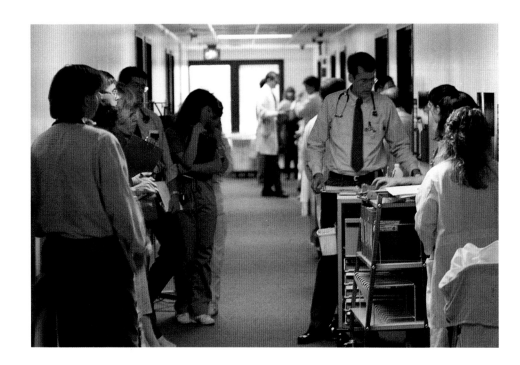

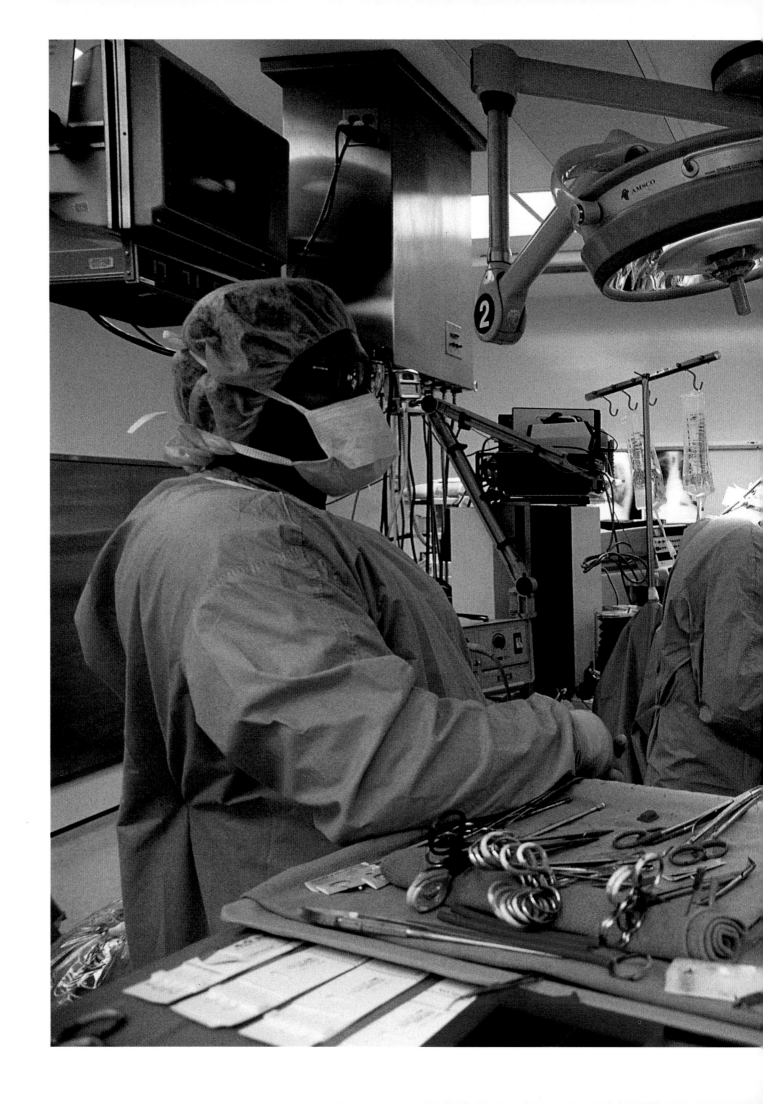

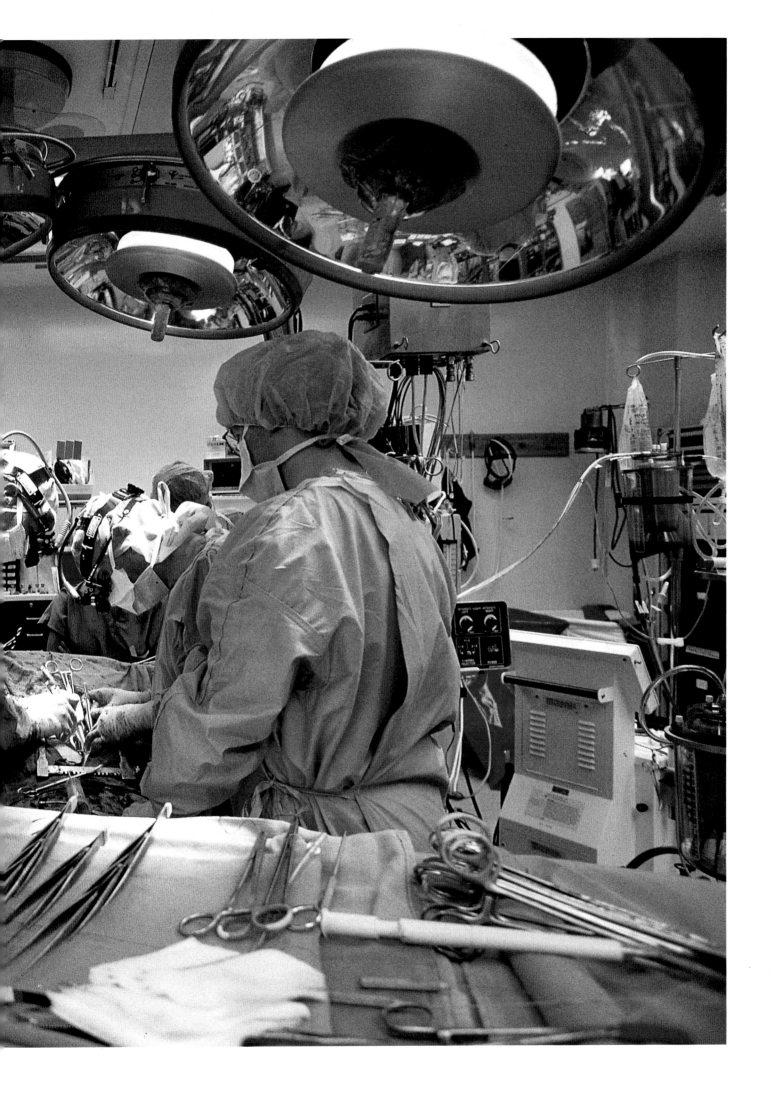

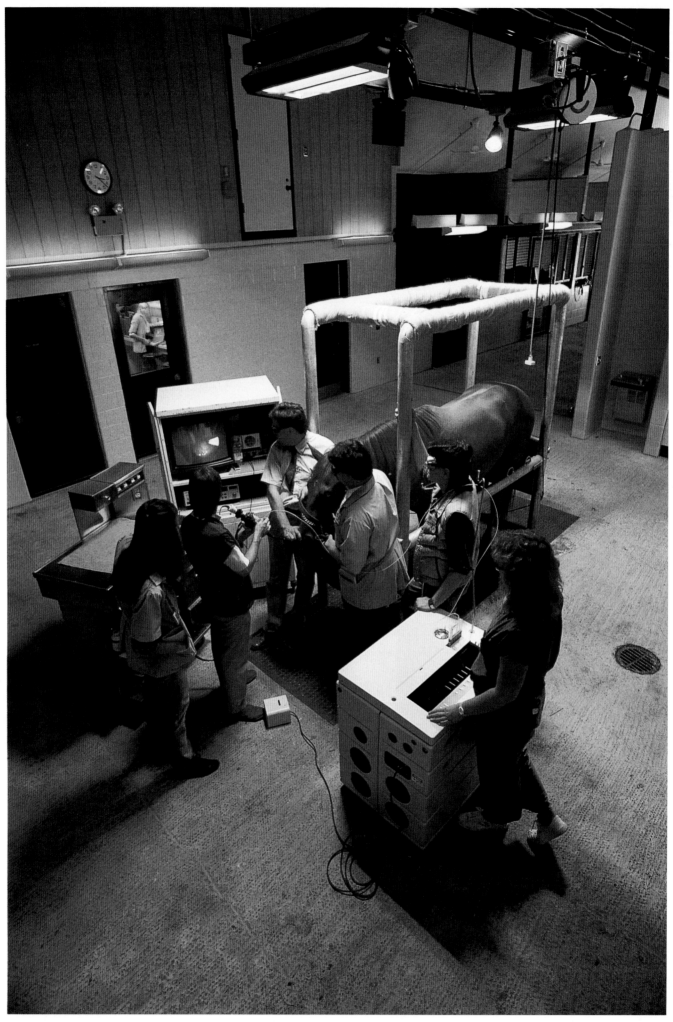

Veterinarian Medical Laboratory

Peabody Hall

The world is our field of endeavor, and we salute every effort in the University to understand that world and to contribute to the solution of its problems.

President J. Hillis Miller

Agriculture Research

We may speak of buildings and equipment and endowment and income, and embody these in our definition of an institution of learning, but the fact remains, as it has been and always will be, that the teaching force is the main element in constituting a school. . .

President Andrew Sledd, Inaugural Address, 1905

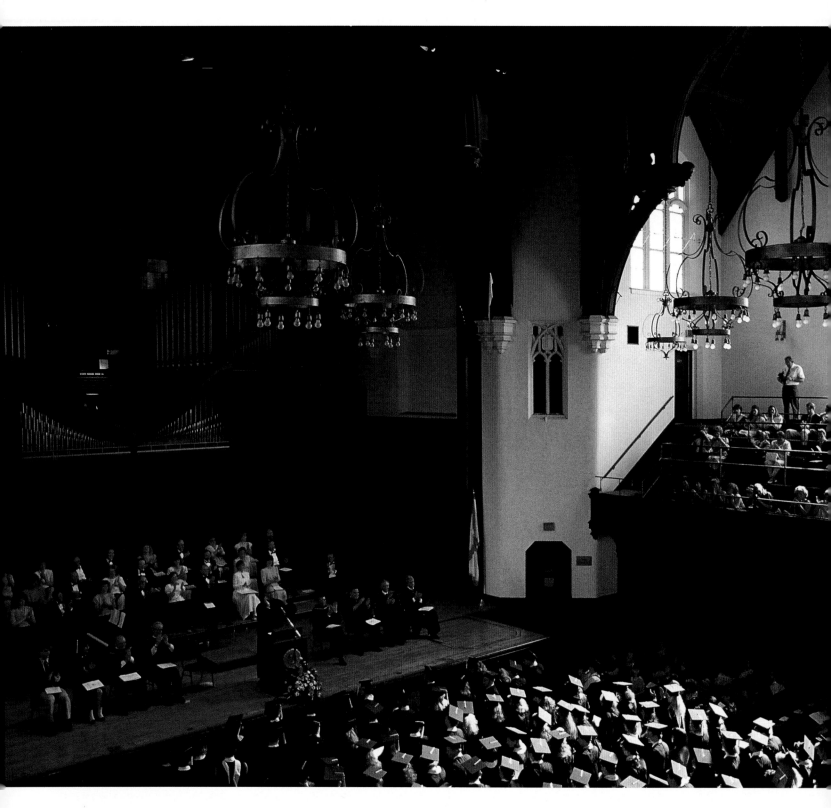

Splendid and exciting as Florida is, never forget that the real treasures of life are people. What I love most about Florida are its people. I hope that you will always put people first, that you will prefer people to objects, and that you will use the knowledge and skills gained here at the University of Florida in the service of people. Achieving success in your chosen field and accumulating a lot of money may be very important goals for some of you at this moment, but later in your lives, if not now, you will realize the ancient truth that only in giving do we receive the goods truly worth possessing: interior peace, sense of purpose, meaning in life.

Manuel Prado Y Colon de Carvajal
Ambassador Extraordinary of Spain, June Commencement, 1981

I do hope that in your much shorter stay here you have come to respect and to cherish this great institution as I do and to be proud of her as I am. Each of you is now an indelible part of her history. Each one of you will contribute to her future and to her reputation . . . by your own accomplishments.

Dr. Alex G. Smith, University of Florida Distinguished Alumni Professor, Commencement, August, 1981

93

In an age of spectators, TV-tuning and body-tuning, we rely on you to go out from the University of Florida as the mind-tuners. We count on you to be the keepers of the culture, the heritage, and the understanding of our civilization. You are the continuing link to the poets and authors who have crystalized civilization's fears and determinations. As students at the University of Florida you have heard the words of poet and writer. Now, as graduates, you are the keepers of that heritage.

Dr. David Chalmers, University of Florida Distinguished Alumni Professor, Commencement, 1986

A LOOK BACK AT THE UNIVERSITY IN PHOTOGRAPHS FROM THE ARCHIVES

An artist's rendering of the University campus of 1916. Although considerably
altered since that time, many of the buildings shown are still part of the campus.

*Our thanks to Dr. Samuel Proctor and the staff of the University Archives for
their help in the creation of this brief photographic review.*

Uncle Dud's College Inn, shown here around 1908, was located across University Avenue, and doubled as the University's first post office.

The foundations of Thomas Hall are laid here in January, 1906. Thomas, Buckman and Machinery Halls were the first three buildings on the Gainesville campus.

Laying sewers and paving the street between the Plaza and Peabody Hall in the 1930s. This may have been a WPA project.

The dirt road behind the Auditorium, looking east to 13th Street. The open lot on the left is the present site of Turlington Hall. To the right is the site of Marston Science Laboratory.

The University Dining Hall, circa 1912. This building, first called the Commons and later Johnson Hall, burned down in 1987.

Buckman Hall (left) and Thomas Hall (right) in the 1920s.

An aerial view of the campus after World War II. The wooden temporary buildings, mostly from Camp Blanding, are scattered around the grounds. Construction in the bottom right corner seems to be the Hub. The circular drive (north) is still visible.

The first section of the Florida Union was finished in 1936 with funds from the WPA and from money raised in the 1920s by William Jennings Bryan. The North wing was completed in 1949. This photo was taken in 1950.

A professor's office, 1920s.

Library East, shown here in 1940, some fifteen years after its completion, was the third library in the University's history. The first library consisted of two rooms in Thomas Hall; the second was located on the second floor of Peabody Hall. The two entrances shown above on the south end of the building were eventually closed off.

The P.K. Yonge Laboratory School and College of Education, shown here in the late 1930s, was completed in 1932. Now called Norman Hall, it was renamed for James Norman, the longtime dean of the College of Education.

Language Hall, now Anderson Hall, (left) and the Library (right) in the 1930s.

The dairy pasture and the barn were located just south of the Auditorium in the 1930s and 1940s. The Architecture Building is now on this site.

This curious photograph from the 1930s is probably not a Moot Court in the College of Law, but a Moot Court skit put on by the law students.

The Law School Library in Bryan Hall, circa 1920s.

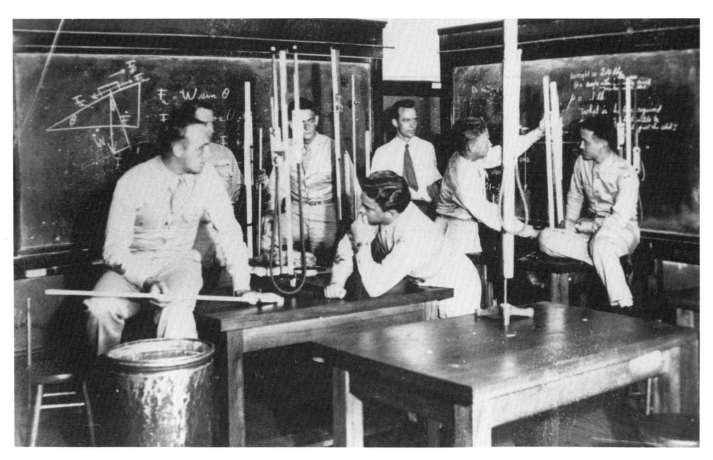

A World War II Officers Candidate School class convenes in the Benton Engineering Building in 1943.

Three Flavet Villages were constructed after World War II to house returning vets and their families. There were three separate housing units, most of which came from Camp Blanding. At right, one of the Flavet Villages, 1947.

The College Inn was the place to be on the campus of the 1950s and early 1960s. Folksingers, inspired by the Kingston Trio and others, were a common sight at the Inn in those days.

Fleming Field was the athletic field for football, baseball, and other outdoor sports in the 1920s. Here a field goal goes over the wooden crossbar as the bleacher-less students stand on the sidelines. Thomas Hall is in the distance.

This was a multi-purpose building in the early part of the century, serving as both a gymnasium and an auditorium (at which William Jennings Bryan spoke). It became the Women's Gymnasium when the University went coed in 1947. The building was completed in 1919, just in time for the New York Giants baseball team to use it as a dressing room before their exhibition game with the Red Sox on Fleming Field.

Big bonfires at football rallies were common in the late 1930s. This bonfire-in-the-making was set up on the Drill Field, now site of the O'Connell Center.

Steve Spurrier quarterbacked, punted and place-kicked for the Gators in 1966 and 1967, and won the Heisman Trophy in 1967. He returned to his alma mater as head coach of the football team for the 1990-91 season.

The Gators, lead by SEC Back-of-the-Week Chuck Hunsinger, beat Georgia 28-7 in 1950.

A Vietnam War protest march at the corner of University Avenue and 13th Street turned a bit ugly in the spring of 1971. Below, Professor Michael Gannon and the police are called to the scene in front of Tigert Hall.

The arch looking toward Thomas Hall, circa 1942. The arch was constructed in 1928.